CRUISE EXCURSIONS

25 of the Best European Cruise Ship and Baltic Cruise Ship Shore Trips

Peter Benn

Argosy Media

Introduction

This is a biased guide based on the real vacations I have taken on cruise ships and the experiences that I've had on my choice of shore excursions. I'm a mature-age traveler and I want to see the most I can in each city but always with the maximum of comfort and the minimum of inconvenience.

I'm not a travel agent. I am just like any paying passenger, someone who has a limited time in a port, wants to see as much as possible at a reasonably economical price and wants to be treated with respect and not just be seen as a commodity to be dumped into an artificial and captive shopping environment. Believe me, this does happen. (Personally, I've seen one too many cameo and leather factory outlets that were part of my shore excursions).

All cruise ships offer much the same list of excursions because each city or town only has a certain number of tourist operators and sites to see.

I can well remember being in Malta at the height of their summer with *nine* cruise ships disgorging passengers during a very short number of hours. We were met at the ship by a coach and taken to where the walking tour began. Whilst we walked for an hour the coach went to another ship and began the whole process over again before picking us up to go to the next site. And so on for the whole nine ships. At least we were staggered and not all in the same site at the one time. These things do happen.

This book is not about saving money by walking down to the quayside and taking whatever tour is on offer from the local peddlers.

It's about choosing the tour offered by the cruise ship company that will interest you the most. One where you will be well looked after, comfortable, and you will see the highlights of the location as promised in the ship's brochure. It will also mean that if you are booked on the ship's excursions then you are *guaranteed* that the ship won't leave port without you. This undertaking by the cruise line for me is a fundamental peace of mind contract. Yes, I may pay more than if I bargain quayside, but I know I am looked after every moment I am away from that ship. I am probably in that port for the one and only time in my life, and going on a port excursion gives me a wonderful taste of what that city and culture has to offer. Invariably you come back to the ship saying that you would have liked to have had more time at so and so, or less time for lunch or more shopping time. It's been my experience that on the second visit, when I went back to a site on my own, I realized that in fact I'd seen just about as much as I needed to see on the ship excursion. The extra benefits from a second visit have been marginal in value and often it misses the 'wow' factor that the first impression can make.

Most of the tours are half day ones of approximately 4-5 hours. This timing is ideal to see the sites, and then, by early afternoon, you are back on the ship to enjoy all the benefits of shipboard life. Alternatively the excursion may offer to drop you in the heart of city or town so that you have a few more hours of shopping or sightseeing. This means that you have to find your own way back to ship and at your own cost. In this scenario the ship will *not* wait for you if you are late. If you are leaving the excursion part way through to do your own thing, make sure that your guide is informed before you do it.

Some of your fellow passengers will object to organized excursions particularly because of the price, and would rather do the sightseeing by themselves. Yes, some (very few) cities are easy to explore on your own and I have listed these at the end of the guide. But unless you are very familiar with the city you are visiting, I believe that a tour is the best and easiest way to see the highlights.

Do yourself a favor – just accept the fact that you will be organized for the whole excursion, you won't be the only tour group visiting that site, occasionally you may have to wait a few minutes for your group's scheduled entry time, and you will be dropped into a shop or location where you wonder what kick-back the operator is making by having you there. These are facts of life about shore excursions – accept them and just thank the universe that you are so privileged to be at that cultural site when so many of the world's population are wondering where their next meal is coming from.

When deciding on your excursion, take note of your expectations of what you want to see and in particular, your physical abilities. Some tours involve a lot of walking over cobblestones and up steps and stairways, so make sure that you have sturdy and comfortable walking shoes and that you have the physical ability to undertake the walks. Some tours will visit religious sites so respect their customs and dress accordingly. Note the amount of free time you will have and where that will be – do you want to eat or shop – it's not easy to do both on most excursions.

Remember also, that as a tourist you are a guest in a new land. Respect the cultural differences and appreciate that things will *not* be the same as they are at home. Toilets and washrooms will be different, food will possibly not be the type or the way that you would cook it, the plumbing is often bizarre by our standards, service in tourist shops may be off-hand or non-existent, aromas in back streets may not always be pleasant. As for me, I like to embrace the differences to my every day life at home. That's why I'm on vacation – to see and experience and enjoy the incredible variety of life that this world offers. On guided ship excursions you will be protected from the extremes of a new and often very different culture so enjoy what is on offer. Such differences make great dinner conversations when you get home.

Headsets are a new phenomenon frequently used on the walking aspects of shore excursions. They enable you to hear everything the guide is telling you without having to be immediately within their reach. You can turn down the volume when the guide becomes too enthusiastic about their local patron saint but it also means that you don't miss the important information about meeting times and pickpocket advice. To me, headsets are a necessary evil. As a photographer, they allow me to be near the group and to hear the history but free enough to take advantage of all the lovely photo opportunities that abound when you stop and look around rather than focusing on the guide. Also take photos from your coach even if the color rendition is tinted. In this digital age much can be done on the home computer to rectify such photos back to natural tones.

And don't try to do too much in one day, as tomorrow you'll probably be in another port and have another tour. In my eyes a cruise vacation should be a balance between shipboard life with all its luxurious pampering and relaxation and seeing something of the ports of call, but knowing that you can't see everything in just a few hours.

Enjoy your travels. I trust that my notes will make your choice an easy and a pleasant one.

Bon voyage!

Ship Board Procedure

Arrival and Check In
When you arrive at the cruise ship my advice is to get there at the beginning of embarkation. This means that you have no last minutes hassles.

Before you leave home and whilst you have access to a computer with a printer, you should book your excursions online and register with the ship your travel details including your credit card details so that all onboard expenses are charged to this card. Remember, that most cruise ships are now cash-free zones with all charges going straight to your credit card via the ship pass you will carry or wear at all times whilst on board.

If your cruise line also offers you online luggage tags, then print them out at home and bring them with you. Don't worry that you will need a stapler to attach the labels to your luggage, as the support staff at the check-in will help you with this.

Carry with you anything you require for a possible two to three hour period between check-in and seeing your luggage again in your cabin. This should include any medicines required. There is no way that you can have access to your luggage during that period.

On arrival, you will need your passport, ship registration details and your luggage tags.

The process begins with a security check of both yourself and your luggage. Once through, if you haven't done so already, you will attach your luggage tags to your bags. This is the last you will see of them until they arrive at your cabin.

You are now given a card to fill in about your health. Any symptoms of colds, flu, vomiting or diarrhea are looked upon as potentially very serious for the ongoing health of all passengers and crew. If you answer "yes" to any of the questions you may be required to have a health check by the ship's doctor before you will be allowed to board.

Then it's a short wait to be called to a counter for the confirmation of your reservation, confirmation of your credit card or other payment arrangement, a photograph taken and the issuing of your ship pass. Usually this will be on a lanyard so that it can hang around your neck.

You then proceed up the gangway, where you will be checked on board by way of the ship pass.

Your stateroom most likely will not be ready, so proceed to the main buffet area where you will be able to enjoy a meal and drinks. From there many tours of the ship begin, and I would advise taking one of these for quick orientation. You will be given a map of the ship at check-in, but to walk the ship is a chance to not only orient yourself as to where everything is, it is also a quiet time to look at the public areas like dining rooms, bars, gymnasium etc without many people using them. You will also be inundated with offers to sign up to everything including spa treatments, specialized restaurants and the Internet (always very expensive).

A call will be made over the public address system when your cabin is ready for occupation. Your luggage may or may not have arrived by this point, but it will do so over the next hour or two. In your stateroom will be your newsletter, your excursion tickets and your cabin attendant introducing him/her self and welcoming you on board.

Unpack, place valuables into the safe (similar to those found in hotel rooms), shower, change – and go to the upper decks for the cocktails and the sail out.

Have a wonderful cruise!

Preparations For An Excursion
All cruise ships vary their going ashore procedure, but this is typical of what I've experienced.

You will be encouraged to purchase your shore excursions online before you begin your cruise. If you do not, then you will be able to purchase the tickets from the Excursion Desk on board. Note that some excursions can sell out and leaving your purchase to the last minute can lead to disappointment.

If you have purchased before boarding, then the tickets will be waiting on the bed in your stateroom on your arrival. I suggest you keep them all secure in your cabin safe.

On the day of the excursion give yourself plenty of time.

My routine is:

- ✓ On the night before prepare what you need to take ashore and write a list noting the extras you need to add the next morning. Recharge those camera and cell phone batteries, find the maps you bought with you, and look through my Check List guide for what else you might need for this particular excursion. I also take photographs of the excursion tickets as this is ideal to incorporate in to your slideshow or video when you get back home. Your ticket is taken from you when you first board the coach to begin the excursion so do this exercise in advance.

- ✓ Be up early to see the arrival in port. This gives you an orientation of what the outward look of the city is like.

- ✓ Have breakfast and maybe a quick few minutes on deck to take in the new day.

- ✓ Then back to the cabin for brushing teeth, visiting the bathroom and checking the list. Double check that you have the right excursion tickets for that day. Put into your

bag the ship's newsletter for that port.
Remember the passport if necessary. And if
you are using your own bottle of water
remember to take it from the refrigerator. Also
any medications – and a final look at the
Check List.

✓ Don't leave your cabin without your ship pass.
You won't get off without it, and your
excursion could leave without you.

Assembling For The Excursion

Most excursions leave from the main assembly area,
usually the theatre. Be there at least 15 minutes before
the scheduled departure time. Only one of your group
should go and register to get the stickers that you will
be required to wear on your clothing throughout the
excursion. If you meet new friends and you all want
to travel on the same excursion and on the same
coach, then again, one person takes all the tickets to
check-in. This ensures that you can all travel together
and have a wonderful shared day with friends.

If you haven't already got your bottle of water now is
the time to purchase it from the stewards in the
theatre.

Each excursion coach is called to depart one at a time.
There may be several coaches going to the same
location, but you will be assigned a particular one,
and that is yours for the day. A staff member will lead
your group to the gangway where you will be security
checked by way of the barcode on your ship pass.

Depending on where you are berthed the coaches may be immediately at the bottom of the gangway or alternatively you may have a long walk along the pier and through the customs building. All the coaches will be waiting in the one area, and your sticker that you are now wearing will indicate which coach is yours. At the point of boarding the coach your guide will take the ticket from you. Seating on the coaches is not allocated.

Your guide will introduce him or herself, so take note of what they look like and are wearing. Whilst on the tour away from the coach they will also carry with them some form of device that you will need to look for in a crowd to indicate your particular group. Often this is a large numeral (the same number as your coach), sometimes, especially with local guides, it can be a distinctive umbrella possibly with a piece of brightly colored ribbon attached to it. Each guide has their own particular means of letting their flock know where they are. If you are to be using audio headsets these will be handed out and tested whilst on the coach going to the first walking section of the tour. Whilst this is happening don't miss out on what is passing your coach window, as often it is scenery or sights that you won't see again.

Arriving Back At The Ship
The coach will bring you as close to the embarkation point as security will allow. When departing the coach most passengers who have had a pleasant excursion like to tip the guide (who will also share it

with the driver). The size of the tip is up to you and how much you feel you have enjoyed your day. There is no obligation to make a tip. (I've seen a day when virtually no-one tipped the combined driver/tour guide because they were all so bored by his incessant and inane chatter. But then another when the guide was so in tune with the passengers and therefore constantly deviated from the usual patter to make the day totally fascinating for their interests, that she was embarrassed by their generosity). You'll know how much, if anything, you might like to give.

You again have to pass through customs and security where your bags and your body will be searched. Remember that most ships do not allow alcohol to be taken aboard for consumption on board. If you do bring it on board it will be confiscated and returned to you at the end of the cruise. Expect delays in this process as often several coaches arrive back at the ship at the same time and the local customs and security officers may be understaffed.

Before you board the ship you may be given a cooling face towel and your hands will be given a squirt of disinfectant. At the top of the gangway you will need to show your ship pass, and your bags and body will again be scanned. Then it's off to your cabin and to a waiting food area.

Excursion Check List

I've now been on over 40 excursions from cruise ships and my experiences suggests that you should consider taking the following with you on your shore excursion:

- ✓ **Your Shipboard Identity Card** – you won't get on or off the ship without this.

- ✓ **Passport and/or Travel Visa** (these are not always necessary and can be a risk to have with you especially in known pickpocket areas. You will be advised if this form of identification is required, particularly for quayside security checks). I always carry a couple of laminated color photocopies of my passport photo page. Put one in your handbag or daypack, one in your wallet, one in your suitcase. I have a friend who also does the same thing with his automobile driver's license. Both are useful for photo identification purposes.

- ✓ **Ship's Daily Newspaper** – this generally includes a basic map of the city, and most importantly, details of sailing time *and* the ship's phone number - very useful information to have should you get into an emergency situation beyond the confines of the excursion.

✓ **Map** – a more detailed map is often a good idea especially in places with winding alleys like Venice.

✓ **Bottle of Water** – water can be hard to come by until well into the tour when shopping time *may* happen. So take a bottle from the ship. Stay hydrated, especially in warmer weather. In Rome the street vendors sell frozen bottles of water in summer – what a fabulous idea.

✓ **Camera** – including a fully charged battery in the camera as well as your spare battery also fully charged. Make it a habit to recharge all batteries overnight. And carry a second storage card. Unexpectedly running out of photo space in the camera is not a happy situation.

✓ **Cell/Mobile Phone** – if you have a global roaming plan with your provider it's very reassuring to have immediate access to the local phone network without having to look for a local public telephone and even more difficult, local coins. Always understand the costs of using your phone in a foreign country, as they can sometimes be horrendous.

✓ **Watch** – you need something on you that will tell you local time. As most shore trips have some free time built in to them you need to know exactly when to meet up with the rest of the group. A hostile coach-load of 40 people who have been left waiting in the heat for you to arrive back late is not a pretty sight. No amount of apologizing will soothe their animosity. Believe me – I've accidentally done it - twice!

✓ **Clothing** – especially if you are visiting religious sites dress accordingly. Women should always be able to cover their shoulders and most of their legs and men should not wear very short shorts. I've not yet seen anyone turned away because of his or her clothing, but respect for the religion is always appreciated. The larger sites often have clothing available such as shawls for women or for men visiting a synagogue a yamaka is usually included in the admission.

And not forgetting:

✓ **Sun Hat, Sunscreen and Sunglasses** – wide brimmed hat for maximum coverage. On some tours there is little shade and a lot of standing in the sun listening to the guide. Peaked caps do not protect the ears or the back of the neck during these often quite substantial periods of time.

✓ **Comfortable Walking Shoes** – break them in well before setting off on your vacation.

✓ **Local Money, Credit Card and/or ATM Card, Money Belt** – it's not wise to carry all your money and identification in the one bag. Spread them around your body and with your traveling companion if you have one. One credit card is usually enough. Leave the others on board. As for local currency, only take what you expect you might spend in a day. And men, under no circumstances carry your wallet in your back hip pocket.

✓ **Medications** - including travel sickness relief.

✓ **Umbrella/Rain Wear** – also pack a plastic bag, as this is very useful for storing a wet jacket or umbrella in.

✓ **Handbag/Daypack** – ladies, don't carry a loose-hanging bag that is easy prey for pickpockets or for theft by a mobile thief as they silently ride by you on their bicycles, scooters or skateboards. Either wear a long-strapped bag diagonally so it hangs in front, or tuck it firmly under your arm. You must make it as difficult as possible for anyone to have access to your bag and/or to be able to cut it from you.

✓ **Swimsuit/Towel** - only take these if your excursion offers an opportunity to swim.

✓ **Additional Clothing** - it's important to pack windproof jackets and woolen clothing if you are going to higher altitudes for the excursion (for example, up Mount Etna).

BARCELONA, Spain

This excursion encompasses both the architectural magnificence of the Barcelona city area together with the nearby iconic **Montserrat Monastery**, along with a touch of the works of the city's most beloved son, **Antoni Gaudi.** If your cruise finishes in Barcelona it is likely that you will be offered the Montserrat excursion as it is an ideal length to fit between your disembarkation early in the morning and the time your hotel will be ready to receive you. Montserrat is a place of peace and tranquility but it is also one of the most highly visited places by Barcelonians and tourists. I visited early in the morning from my cruise ship and consequently we were one of the few coaches there. It was indeed peaceful, the early morning mists were disappearing as the sun warmed the air, and we had no waiting to see the **Black Madonna**, the patron-virgin of Catalonia. By the time we left late morning the coach bays were all full.

View from Gaudi's Guell Park

La Sagrada Família

The Excursion
The journey to Montserrat is around an hour, and
takes you through the wide and leafy boulevards of
the city of Barcelona. On the outskirts you begin a
journey that winds its way high up into the mountains

to some 4,000 feet. Montserrat Monastery is perched on a magnificent rocky outcrop and was founded back in the 11th century. Here the monks in residence continue the Order's thousand year worship and prayer vigils. If you can be there before the bulk of the day's visitors arrive you will appreciate the spirituality that pervades the area. For me it was a privilege to soak in the peace and harmony.

You then return to Barcelona via a different route across the spectacular **Montserrat Mountain Ridge** and down into the city. Here you will enjoy a visit to the Cathedral of **La Sagrada Familia**, a work in progress since 1892 encompassing the outpourings from the very fertile and imaginative visionary, Gaudi. It's like no other building on earth, and until you stand inside it (construction site it still may be) you simply can't imagine the size or the sense of majesty it commands. When completed it will rank with the great architectural wonders of our world. It's a must-see for every visitor to this great city. Three other works of this master are also well worth visiting – **Guell Park, Casa Batllo** and the amazing curved residential building **La Pedrera (Casa Mila).**

If you are only slightly adventurous, the hop-on, hop-off buses (there are three routes), offer an economical and fun way to see the city and suburban sights on your own. They are clean, well run, visit all the important places, are frequent, reliable and are always extremely busy. A good starting point is the very centrally located **Placa de Catalunya.** By taking one or more of these buses you will see and enjoy more than perhaps you would with a more formal excursion organized from your ship. This is one city where this type of tourist bus service is par excellence. Perhaps enjoy the organized Montserrat morning excursion but then do your own thing for the rest of the day. In summer when it is very hot don't forget a wide brimmed hat, sunscreen and plenty of bottled water. Riding on the top open-area of these buses gives the best view but you are also exposed to the full extremes of the relentless sun.

The local train system is extremely good and easy to use. A 45-minute train ride to **Sitges** is well worthwhile. Sitges is a lovely old town with specialty shops, food outlets and cool earthy walkways. But it is the beach everyone comes to see and enjoy. It's also the mecca for European gay men.

Remember also that in summer it stays light until well into the evening, and being on Barcelona time, the evening meal might not begin until well after 11pm. When you stroll along the **La Rambla** (and everyone does) beware of pickpockets – day or night. Their reputation in this street is known the world over. Having said that, this amazing street is at its best late in the evening. Filled with happy people going nowhere in particular it's a great place to amble, eat, stop for a drink or an ice-cream, watch the many talented street performers and know that you are in a happy place that is so different from being home. These are the times that refresh the tiredness of the soul and remind you that this is a good reason to travel – to experience the differences that make cultures so fascinating and enjoyable.

My Recommendation
Unlike many other cities where the comfort and security of an excursion organized from the ship makes for easy viewing, Barcelona is a place where you could be comfortable about doing some of your own touring. English is widely spoken and the inhabitants enjoy life with an infectious passion. Do the Montserrat tour, and then join up with a couple of other cruise friends and go together to explore via the hop-on, hop-off buses. And don't forget to sample the magnificent food, including the amazing variety of tapas. This is an architecturally grand city with an enthusiasm for life to match. Indulge yourself and feel your soul re-energized.

The beach suburb of Sitges

BILBAO, Spain

Guggenheim Museum

There is one main reason for a shore excursion into
Bilbao – the **Guggenheim Museum**. This is a world-
revered piece of architecture from the American
architect Frank Gehry. It sits in this industrial city like
a sparkling silver dewdrop from another world. The
surface is in fact titanium. With its curves and spaces
and soaring atrium it is a wonder of modern
engineering and design. Inside there are both
permanent and temporary exhibitions. Don't overlook
taking a look at *Puppy*, a giant terrier dog designed by
Jeff Koons and covered in living vegetation. For
Bilbao, this statue close to the Museum's entrance has
become the city's iconic image. A walk in the nearby
old city centre is pleasant but hardly memorable.

CADIZ (Seville), Spain

The port of Cadiz is the entry for a full day excursion to Seville. The trip to and from Seville takes around two hours each way, but seeing Seville as a taste of the architectural beauties of Spain is an undeniable pleasure.

Alcazar Palace

The Excursion

You drive through the port streets of Cadiz and then on through the cork plantations to **Seville**. Everywhere you look is history, particularly the stunning Moorish architecture. Your tour guide will be busy pointing out the **Torre del Ora** (the Tower of Gold), the **Plaza de Toros de la Maestranza** (the bullring), the ancient city walls, the gardens, the **Universidad** (the female cigar makers were the inspiration for the opera *Carmen*), references to the historical figure of El Cid and many beautiful and historic buildings. The exquisite glazed ceramic tile decorations are in abundance and as you will see throughout the day, are a feature of the architecture of this beautiful city.

Your excursion is very likely to include these three sites:

The Alcazar Palace Complex – here you will be transported back to the Moorish fort that it originally was. Superb and lavish wall decorations of tiles, a beautiful reflective pool, wonderfully manicured serene gardens, vaulted hallways and cool covered walkways make this complex comparable to the better known Alhambra at Granada. This is a treat not to be missed. If your tour does not include this complex, then take your shopping time to explore it. You won't be disappointed.

Seville Cathedral (Cathedral Of Saint Mary Of The See) – this is the third largest church in the world and the largest Gothic one. It is vast, impressive, very ornate – and the burial place of Christopher Columbus. The construction of the bell tower (**La Giralda Tower**) began in 1184 and is a joyous mixture of several faiths and art periods.

Plaza de Espana (Spain Square) – this was a vast semi-circular building constructed for an exposition in 1929. It contains a huge number of historical scenes and alcoves that represent different provinces of the country. These images are made up entirely of stunning ceramic tiles. If you have an interest in the decorative arts you'll soon discover this building is a joy to amble around.

My Recommendation

Vacations are about seeing things that are different to what we have at home. The Moorish architecture of Seville is a world away from modern western architecture. It's exotic, beautiful, creative and responsive in style to the hot climate. You are guaranteed a splendid day that is a feast for the eyes and enrichment for your artistic soul. Don't miss it!

Giralda Tower (left) and Seville Cathedral

CIVITAVECCHIA (Rome), Italy

Rome is one place you have to see at least once in your lifetime as there is so much history to experience. Any excursion from a cruise ship can therefore be limited to only a few particular sites. There will always be many, many more days worth of history to discover, so whatever excursion you choose, it will simply be a delectable taste of more to come.

The Roman Forum

The Excursion

Firstly, the port of Rome is **Civitavecchia**. This is some 45-60 minutes away from the heart of Rome so an excursion means anything up to two hours of the trip will be getting there and back. Hence many of the excursions are very long (10 hours plus).

Secondly, dress conservatively as you will almost certainly be visiting religious areas. Knees and shoulder coverings are recommended.

I suggest an excursion that takes in the **Vatican Museum** and **St Peter's Basilica** together with time at the **Colosseum** would be ideal for the first time visitor. If you are visiting in summer the crowd numbers are huge with very long wait times to enter. Your excursion will have scheduled entry times and waiting periods will be minimum but prepare yourself for mass tourism, especially inside the Vatican Museum. Here you will see items from their huge and unique depository ranging from maps, statues and paintings through to icons, relics, more statues and wonderful frescoes. At your appointed time the guide will take you into the **Sistine Chapel** (no photos allowed but that doesn't seem to stop it happening. I've never seen so many innocently carried mobile tablets facing skyward in my life). The visit will be brief and then it's out to the vast **St Peter's Square** and into **St Peter's Basilica.** This is a huge edifice and for anyone of the Roman Catholic faith this is a particularly poignant moment. But be warned: the gypsies know this and work the area whilst tourists have let down their guard. They are very skilled at stealing, so always be vigilant and keep your fellow group members alert. You will leave the area after crossing the Square and depart by coach.

Inside the Vatican Gardens

The **Colosseum** is one of those iconic structures that has to be seen to be believed. Walking on a guided tour of the building brings it vividly to life and you may well imagine yourself back two thousand years. There are museum pieces on show which are often overlooked by the guides. They are well worth getting up close and personal to. And oh yes, the infamous young men dressed as Centurians who offer themselves for a photo opportunity with you. Remember that if you do, then after the photo is taken it will be ten Euro cash – immediately, no argument, and they don't take no for an answer. Any tour of Rome will also drive you past sites like the **Forum**, the **River Tiber, Circus Maximus,** the **Arch of Constantine**, the **Spanish Steps** and the **Victor Emmanuel Monument**.

It's unlikely you'll see the **Trevi Fountain** as this is in an area that a coach can't access so a stop would be necessary to allow you to throw your coin. Neither will you see the **Pantheon** for the same reason unless there is a walking component to your excursion. If there is then these two attractions along with the **Piazza Navona** will be an added bonus to your glorious day in the eternal city.

My Recommendation

Anything you see in Rome adds to your accumulated cultural heritage. So whatever you choose there will be so much more that you could have seen. In summer Rome is hot and crowded, so be forewarned that at times it will feel like the whole world has descended on the city at the one time. If it's hot, don't try to see too much as it's very exhausting. In summer look for the roadside street merchants who will sell you a frozen bottle of water. It continues to stay refreshing for an hour or two and is ideal for the on-the-move tourist. At the end of the day you'll be exhausted, but hopefully inspired by the history you have witnessed and will be eager to start planning for your return journey.

COPENHAGEN, Denmark

This delightful small-scale city could very well weave a special place in to your heart. There's a feeling here about community, about enjoying life at the human level, about being in touch with the ideals of humanity and the environment. There are smiles here, and friendliness that is often missing from the intensity of life of larger cities. In Copenhagen there is that feeling of not chasing the wealth dreams that some larger cities offer, but rather of a peaceful and vibrant enjoyment of friends, family and neighbors. As a tourist you will be made very welcome in to this community. A bonus is that in summer it is still light until 10.30pm or later and though this will throw into chaos your body clock, it gives a lot more time for seeing the sights. It's also very flat, so walking is relatively easy.

Nyhaven

The Excursion

I stayed in Copenhagen for five days before boarding my cruise ship. These are some of the places I visited that you will find on many shore excursion offerings…

The Little Mermaid – set in delightful gardens that will remind you of England this little statue (and it is little), is the most photographed icon in the country. So expect other people to crowd into your cherished photos. The park also has the **Kastellet** and **Frihedsmuseet**, the remains of a 16th century fortress and a museum to the Danish Resistance Movement of World War 2. (Note: most tours will only give you time to see the Little Mermaid).

Amelienborg – four beautiful Rococo buildings where some of the Danish royal family reside. There is a changing of the guard at noon.

Nyhaven – Copenhagen is a maritime city, and this canal is a bustle of boats, restaurants, tourists and shops. Day or night it is the beating heart of the city. Look for the cream colored house at Number 67 as the writer **Hans Christian Andersen** lived there for nineteen years.

Canal Cruise - Nyhaven is also where the hour long canal cruises depart from and return to. A cruise is a wonderful way to see much of the city. Highlights will include getting up close to the Little Mermaid (makes a great photo of everyone else trying to photograph her from the land), the new **Opera**

House, canal sections that will remind you of Amsterdam, the amazing external spiral staircase on **Von Frelsers Kirke**, quaint little bridges and many historic public buildings.

Tivoli Gardens – whether or not you care for amusement parks, this is one place that is an absolute 'must see'. It's a vibrant mixture of old world amusement rides and today's carnival attractions, spectacular gardens, lawns and flowerbeds, color everywhere, restaurants and eating places, live entertainments and in every way a fantasy escape like nowhere else. This was a forerunner to the Disney parks and is a totally enjoyable escapist few hours for adults and children alike. Don't miss spending some time here.

Rosenborg Slot – set in the midst of beautiful gardens, this castle contains the famous Danish Crown Jewels as well as a myriad of fascinating rooms filled with trinkets, furniture, portraits and art. The Jewels are available for viewing for an additional admission price and they are spectacular and easy to view close-up. This castle is always popular with tourists and locals alike.

Rundetarn – The Round Tower has a cobblestone spiral ramp that turns on itself some seven times before the top. Splendid views of the city from the world's oldest still functioning observatory at the top.

My Recommendation

An organized excursion will show you the highlights of the city, but it is an easy city to walk around and explore so if you are the slightest bit adventurous you can see much by foot and canal – and especially by bicycle. One warning: the citizens use bicycles like Americans use cars. There are cycle lanes everywhere. Be aware of them and do not walk on them or cross them without looking both ways. Cyclists are very possessive of their lanes and they do not take kindly to tourists standing on them. Oh, and wear sturdy walking shoes – there are cobblestones everywhere!

The Little Mermaid and her admirers

CORFU (Kerkira), Greece

We've all seen the photos of the whitewashed walls of other almost tree-less Greek islands, but that is not what Corfu is about. Corfu offers vacationers history, beautiful beaches, villas nestled in lovely treed environments, a very active marine-based lifestyle, olive and citrus groves, historic mansions and should you need it, even a game of English cricket. Yes, it's a wonderful mix of culture, cuisine and architecture - a legacy of their many rulers – Byzantine, Venetian, French and the British.

Vlacherna Monastery on Mouse Island

The Excursion

Remembered to pack a towel and swimwear as it's likely that your tour information won't tell you that there is a 45-minute stop at one of the most beautiful little beaches. Your tour begins with a scenic drive around the old but still very bustling **Corfu Town** and harbor. Then walk around the narrow colorful streets, often underneath the drying washing strung across the street by the occupants living above. Spend a few moments at the **Church of St. Spiridon**, so named after the patron saint of the island. Locate the **Liston,** a copy of the Rue de Rivoli in Paris and have a coffee. Shopping is easy and plentiful here. On the rest of the tour it will be difficult or non-existent.

Then back on to the coach to rise upwards through the town to **Kanoni** for a splendid view of the **Vlacherna Monastery** situated on **Mouse Island**, one of the most photographed places in all of the Mediterranean. Its setting is stunningly beautiful. All tours will stop here to let you take photos. It's the iconic holiday photo to make others back home envious.

Then it's a 30-minute journey through wooded hillsides to **Paleokastritsa's Monastery**. Built in 1226 it's a charming small church complete with icons, sacred books and a variety of cats that laze in the shade of the vines and the archways. It's situated on a cliff which has at its base one of the most beautiful and iconic beaches you will find anywhere in the world. It's small, overcrowded but the water is crystal clear. A swim or a paddle here will definitely be one of the absolute highlights of your entire vacation. The stop may also give you time to be taken by the local guides in a rowboat to the nearby grotto. Then, it's back over the island to return to your ship.

My Recommendation

The Greek islands are particular favorites of many cruise guests. Corfu is a wonderful mix of cultures, history, architecture, beaches and food. It is sun drenched, beautiful and relaxing. It's like being on a permanent vacation. Little wonder that many, many travelers keep returning to this remarkable corner of the world. I loved my day in Corfu and it's definitely on my bucket list for a longer return visit.

Sun drenched street in the Old Town

HELSINKI, Finland

Today your excursion ashore will be low key and relaxing. Helsinki is reasonably compact, friendly and very clean. There's an air of quiet confidence and pride that emphasizes a culture that has made its own mark in the world by doing things their own way whilst under difficult political systems over the centuries.

Senate Square and Lutheran Cathedral

The Excursion

I trust that you will have a most memorable day like I did. This is not because of the buildings we saw, but it was the people we met. The tour begins with a coach trip around the city and the port area. This ends on **Senate Square** where you will get to see the elegant **Lutheran Cathedral**. You need to be able to walk up many steep steps to get to it. If you've just been to St Petersburg on your cruise, then this relatively austere Cathedral will be a total contrast to those in the Russian city. You may also get to see the famous **Rock Church** that was carved into solid rock, before it's off to the countryside for a very pleasant 30-minute journey to **Sipoo**. Here you'll enjoy a few minutes at **St Sigfrid's Church**, dating back to the 15th century. You're literally in the middle of the countryside so take in the fresh air.

A short journey down meandering back roads past the summer wildflowers and you come to the end of the little valley. Here a wonderful husband and wife team will invite you in to their home for traditional berry cake and coffee. Yes, the entire coach-load of some 30 people can spread throughout the house, look at the family sauna, meander in the garden and sit on the deck. It's a unique and heartwarming experience to be made so welcome and to actually be in a home complete with all the family memorabilia and collected souvenirs. Then go on a short walk up a small hill from where you'll see a beautiful lake and a traditional sauna complete with a little jetty to run out on and jump into the lake. As you return to Helsinki, you realize you have just met two of the most welcoming, friendly and fun people. And perhaps their smile and joviality will linger in your memory far longer than any architecture you might see on your cruise.

My Recommendation

This excursion was possibly the most relaxing of any that I have done anywhere. But it was the journey to the countryside and the meeting of the family that made it memorable. With shore excursions from cruise ships we tend to enjoy the city sights because of their closeness and convenience, and in doing this we tend not to meet any locals other than the tour guide and the souvenir seller. With this tour the countryside is only 30-minutes away and it gives you a satisfying mix of both city and rural life. And – you get to chat with the locals and see at close quarters how they live. If you like relaxed touring this one is memorable.

The family home in the Finnish countryside that welcomes coach tour visitors

IBIZA, Spain

Waterfront Cafes

Any excursion that begins with a visit to a saltpan can only get better as the tour goes on. And with my tour, so it did. There has been nothing quite as surreal on any of my other excursions to match a coach-load of barely awake passengers peering out of the windows at the deadly dull image of an evaporating **saltpan**. Fortunately the next stop was **Jesus**, a village in the hinterland where a small 16th century church is on display. Then down into the old quarter of **Ibiza** and a look at the waterfront. There's money on show here in the marina, but also on show are the very hung-over and wasted young folk who are much the worse for wear after a heavy night (or is that week) of partying and drinking. After all, this is party central for the youth of Europe. Then it was up to the citadel that overlooks the harbor. This fine old bastion, the 16th century **Portal de ses Taules**, is worth a look, and gives a fine view of the harbor and an opportunity to photograph your ship from a high angle. Then go back to your ship and enjoy the amenities. And if like me on a future cruise your ship happens to berth here again – I suggest you do as I did and stay on board!

View of Ibiza from Portal de ses Taules

IZMIR (Ephesus), Turkey

Today's excursion to the ruins of **Ephesus** will be a grand one. These are some of the best Roman ruins to be found anywhere, especially in Eastern Europe, and to walk among them will give you a great sense of history. They are remarkably well preserved, and through their sheer size and complexity exude the majesty and glory that was the Roman Empire. Because of their importance there are always huge numbers of tourists here, so expect some possible crowding along the main street. The site is large and well managed with all visitors moving in the same direction, so this allows ample opportunity for each visitor to enjoy any and everything they'd like to inspect. The route is approximately 2 miles (3 kms) in length over rough stones – and there is no shade.

The Excursion

Most tours to Ephesus will begin with a visit to the hilltop location of **Meryemana**, located some 5 miles (8 kms) from the ruins, to see the **House of the Blessed Virgin (**aka **Mary's House** and **House of the Virgin Mary).** After leaving **Izmir** the journey is through fertile farmlands, past hilltop castles followed by a steady climb upwards. The coach will park in an area that allows for a short walk to the House. As the welcoming sign indicates, this House "and its surroundings is a sacred and holy place. While visiting, please observe silence and be decently (and) appropriately dressed". For those of the Christian and Muslim faiths this is an important and revered site.

House of the Blessed Virgin

The House is considered to be the last home of the
Blessed Virgin, the Mother of Jesus Christ. **The
Chapel,** which is built on the site of the original
house, is regarded as the first basilica in the world to
be dedicated to the Blessed Virgin. Amidst the strong
commercialism that is present here, there is also
serenity and dignity enhanced by its nature park
atmosphere. On the day I visited there was choral
singing and an outdoor Mass was being celebrated.
There is also a wall for prayer notes and blessings and
areas where you can sit quietly to meditate. You'll
possibly have a brief wait to enter the House and once
inside the simple structure you'll have time for a short
prayer whilst standing – but *no photos* – they are very
strict on that. There is little to actually see other than
a well attended altar, but rather it's the spiritual
connection to its history that is so special for the
believers. Many of our group purchased pre-stamped
envelopes to post back to loved-ones as well as
additional religious icons for gifts. There is evidence
of healings that have resulted from drinking the

waters of the spring. Whether pilgrim or tourist, you will find a calmness and serenity here that, at least for a short time, is an all too rare occurrence on other cruise excursions. The only day to avoid visiting is August 15, the Feast of the Assumption of Mary.

As the coach travels down the hill towards Ephesus it will possibly briefly stop at a large **golden statue of the Virgin** on the left-hand side of the road. So if you want a photo, make sure you are sitting on the left side, as most coaches don't allow passengers to disembark for a photo shoot.

Your journey through the **Ephesus** ruins is down an easy gradient that allows for plenty of side diversions to see something in more detail. There is virtually no shade along the way so it's time to put on the sunglasses, the wide-brimmed hat and carry your bottle of water. Our tour had umbrellas that, whilst bulky to use were great to stand under during the inevitably long discourses your guide will give you. Whatever time of the year you are there, these are prerequisites. And be very careful with your wallet and valuables, especially at the crowded entrance area and whilst moving in groups.

The walk along the main path begins at the **Baths of Varius** and ends at the stunning **Library of Celsus**. Along the way see **The Odeon** meeting place (like a mini-theatre) and pass through the **Gates of Hercules** into the impressive **Curetes Street**. See examples of **Doric, Ionic and Corinthian columns** (look for 3 free-standing columns next to one another that show the three types), marvel at statues, photograph the cats as they sleep in the sun, admire the mosaic floors and the murals on the walls of the homes of the wealthy, check out the community toilets the Romans shared, peruse the brothel area …..

Typical summer morning in Curetes Street

– then look toward the magnificent **Library of Celsus**, one of the world's most beautiful architectural ruins…..

This is your quintessential Roman ruins photo opportunity and is often the backdrop for a group photo. Walk up the steps and admire the sheer size and grandeur of the building and then inside, just sit for a moment in the shade and contemplate the wonders of this site. Outside again look at the **four statues** in the front – Sophia (wisdom), Arete (virtue), Ennoia (intellect) and Episteme (knowledge).

Our walk then continues past the **Agora** (marketplace) and up to the huge **Theatre**. Climb up a row or two and imagine watching a play or hearing music played on a summer's night. It's a wonderful structure.

The tour ends a short walking distance further on in the bedlam of the modern day market place where your every need for a souvenir will be met – including my favorite - "Genuine Fake Watches"!

Some tours may also include on the way back to the ship a visit to a **carpet factory or co-operative**. If so, these can in fact be surprisingly interesting with hot tea, cool drinks and a presentation of the carpets in a stunningly choreographed style that owes much to a Broadway show. Be aware that any indication from you of interest in a carpet could have the aggressive salesman persistently keeping you company and making tempting price offers to you. Should you purchase a carpet then freight will generally be free (paid by the Turkish authorities) and you will sign the back of the carpet so that you will know it's yours when it arrives at your home. The carpets I saw that day on a co-operative near Ephesus were by far the best I have seen anywhere.

My Recommendation

Though probably hot, dusty and exhausting, your day in Ephesus will definitely be one to remember. There's a wonderful sense of size and grandeur, of history and a very special glimpse into another civilization. When you realize that only some 20% of the site has be unearthed one can only imagine what other treasures will eventually be exposed. For those who want to see more of what has been unearthed and taken from the site you need to visit **Vienna** and spend a day at the **Ephesos Museum**.

Welcome to Izmir

ISTANBUL, Turkey

One full-day excursion is simply not enough time to get to know this magnificent and bustling city. You need many days, and you need to be able to explore it on foot. It's big, grand, historic, and culturally diverse. There's the harbor, the mosques, the markets, the grand vistas, the palaces, the street life. Here you can absorb life being lived in all its amazing diversity. It's safe, well organized and a photo opportunity around every corner.

Berthed Cruise Ships as seen from the Ferry Terminal

The Excursion

Today will be a full one so prepare your self for sensory overload. You travel into the old city along narrow winding streets wondering if the coach will be able to navigate them successfully. First stop is the 1400 year old, **St Sophia's Basilica (Haghia Sophia).** As you step off the coach you will have your first encounter with the many street sellers who will constantly find you at all the tourist meeting points trying to interest you in their souvenir guide books. Inside the mosque be amazed at the enormity of it and the stunning mosaic decorations. Go to the first level and look down as this will give you a great sense of the size of the building. Nearby is the **Blue Mosque** with its beautiful Iznik tiles. This mosque is a working one, so at certain times it will be closed for prayer. It's also shoes off for everyone, and for women, a head covering. The other must-see building, or more correctly, series of buildings, is the magnificent **Topkapi Palace**. After a short walk through the grounds you get to see the magnificent jewels and the wonderful architecture. Just along from the Treasury get your camera ready for a stunning view across the **Bosphorus.** Also walk across to the opposite side of the complex near the **Harem** where you will get another stunning photo opportunity, this time of the city including the berthed cruise ships and the **Galata Tower**.

The day is not complete without a cruise on the harbor. They are approximately one and a half to two hours long, and you will see fabulous views, be amazed at the incredible amount of water traffic, pass under stunning modern bridges, see palaces and old military academies, fortresses, modern mansions, and if you are there in summer, you'll see life being lived along the water's edge with swimming, fishing and picnics. If your excursion includes a meal of traditional meats, dips and drinks then that is a bonus that will make this whole day totally memorable. Through exhaustion and sensory overload you will sleep well tonight.

Other places to see if you have the time include:

Dolmabahce Palace – go on an organized tour otherwise you could have a very long wait for entry. No photos inside. Wonderful views of the water.

Panorama 1453 History Museum– you won't find this on excursions, but it is easy to get to by tram. Imagine a huge dome under which you stand in the middle. All around you a battle takes place complete with cannons, battle noise and other real objects. The dome is painted with huge action sequences, so the result is you are standing in a battlefield with a feeling of being there. Very few of these panoramas exist in the world, so this is an experience that any history buff would thoroughly enjoy.

Basilica Cistern and/or **Cistern Of 1001 Columns** – see how water was stored nearly 2000 years ago. Very clean, well run and not at all frightening for those who don't like going even slightly underground.

Sirkeci Station – very few travelers seem to know about this lovely station built specially for the fabled Orient Express train. There's a small museum and a place to get a snack. The waiting room will transport you back to an earlier grander era of train travel. Conveniently located near the ferry terminal.

Grand Bazaar – a visit here should be on everyone's list of things to see and do. It's vast, labyrinthine, bulging with things to buy and it's all under cover.

You can easily get lost so carrying a map is a good idea. You will also be hassled to enter the stores but don't take this too seriously – it's all part of the ritual to get you to buy. If you do enter the shop you'll probably be offered a drink of hot apple tea, a discovery that I am still enjoying back at home. I can practically guarantee that you won't leave the bazaar empty-handed, as something unexpected will tempt you to purchase. Also get your guide, or a trusted shopkeeper known to the guide, to explain the minimum price the trader will take for the item. Once you know this detail you will be able to see from the code on the price tag the minimum price acceptable after the haggling. If you're buying an expensive item, this is good knowledge to be armed with. But not every guide will know or share this inside knowledge with you. If your tour takes you to an expensive shop as an introduction to the bazaar then that is a good time to ask.

Spice Market – this is rich with color, tradition and a feeling of exotica. Not as crowded as the Grand Bazaar.

Suleymaniye Mosque – slightly off the well-worn tourist route but still within walking distance of all the Old Town sites, this working mosque is a delight. Women will need to cover their head and shoulders.

Ayasofya Hamam – this is a stunningly restored 16th century Turkish Bath located between Haghia Sophia and the Blue Mosque. Go for both the architecture and the exquisite luxury of being pampered.

My Recommendation

On your day in Istanbul try to see a mosque, visit the Topkapi Museum, shop at the Grand Bazaar and find time to take a cruise. These four activities will give you a diverse glimpse at this amazing culture. It may well also tell you that you will need to return to see much more and perhaps also go out on a tour to other parts of Turkey. Don't stay on board your cruise ship today – Istanbul is one of the great cities of the world and will be a highlight of your vacation. See as much as you possibly can. Tomorrow you can sleep.

Interior Haghia Sophia

LA CORUNA (Corunna), Spain

Tower Of Hercules

This city is in Northern Spain and on the day I visited
in September was wet and windswept. It is situated on
a peninsula and quite exposed to the climate
variations. Its history includes the Normans, Vikings,
Romans and Spanish so it is long established as a
marine base and trading city. The half day tour
included a visit to a beach, the **Tower Of Hercules** (a

2,000 year old lighthouse built in Roman times), a walk through part of the **Old Town** and the offer of a tourist tram ride. This was followed by a drive along Europe's longest promenade finishing at the summit of **Mount of San Pedro Park** from which there is a panoramic view of the city and the ocean. These sites are widely spaced apart and don't easily lend themselves to self-discovery, so an organized excursion is recommended.

My Recommendation

You will also possibly be offered an all day excursion to the church of **Santiago de Compostela** that is at the end of the **Way Of St James** pilgrim walk in Santiago. The city is now a UNESCO World Heritage site. Do that one in preference to a half day in La Coruna.

Local tourist tram

LA SPEZIA (Le Cinque Terre), Italy

La Spezia is the port of call in Northern Italy that is the gateway to the stunningly beautiful **Cinque Terre** villages. The whole village area is now a UNESCO national park. The ideal way to see these villages is to arrive from the sea, walk between at least two of the villages (subject to closure from rock falls and floods) and then return to La Spezia by road. The day will be a feast for photo enthusiasts and will be memorable for the quaintness and color of the villages.

Corniglia

The Excursion

If it's summer, pack your bathing costume, towel and sun lotion (a time for swimming may not be mentioned in the activities of the excursion but on my tour we had an unexpected two hours to fill in), wear a wide brimmed hat and carry a bottle of water. You will leave the ship by tender and travel into the foreshore where your cruiser will be waiting to take

59

you out to sea, around **Pontovenere** and on to the
first of the five villages – **Riomaggiore**. Disembark
here to begin the coast walk (the **Via dell'Amore**) to
the next town of **Manarola**. The path clings
seemingly precariously to the steep hillside with the
ocean below you on your left. You'll also see huge
numbers of padlocks that have been fastened to
various parts of the fencing as lovers' tributes to each
other. This is after all, a pathway dedicated to lovers.
After about 30 minutes you'll reach Manarola and
time for a drink break.

Here you'll re-board a vessel to take you the 10-
minutes to **Corniglia**. Have cameras at the ready as
you disembark, as this is a quintessential village with
a beautiful beach and color everywhere. You may be
told to include lunch in your 45-minute stop here. My
advice is to ask how long you will be at the next town
(possibly up to two hours) as it might be better to
photograph here and eat at the next village.

Then it's back on the water to travel to **Vernazzo**
where you will say goodbye to the water component
of your day. This village is very relaxed, has a nice
beach, nice uncrowded places to eat and drink, and is
a good location to have that swim (time permitting).
What your guide might not tell you is that to the west,
around the small cliff where you walked in to the
village, is the resort town of **Monterosso.** You walk
through a small tunnel and there before you is
everything typical of a Mediterranean resort – hotels,
what seems like thousands of umbrellas on the beach,
shops, food outlets, and huge numbers of tourists. The

two places could not be more chalk and cheese. So whichever lifestyle suits you best, have two hours of indulgent sunshine, swimming, eating, drinking and fun. You will then walk through Monterosso to a waiting coach, which will wind its way to the top of the steep hillside to the road that clings to it. Once on this road there is not much to see until you return to the lovely port of La Spezia.

My Recommendation
If at all possible arrive at Cinque Terre by water. Like the fabled Amalfi Coast area this means gives you the best possible view of the area. Prepare for the fact that you may not be able to do the walk between the towns because of rock falls and other reasons for closure, and if the sea is rough, you will be transported both ways by coach, or coach and train combination. Carry a bottle of water with you, wear comfortable shoes and a brimmed hat, take any seasickness requirements with you, pack a bathing costume and towel and enjoy the beauty of this unique part of the world. Talk to the guide at the start of the tour and find out precisely what the itinerary is so that you can plan accordingly for swimming, food and shopping.

Monterosso

LE HAVRE (Mont-St-Michel), France

You don't need an excuse to go to Mont-St-Michel. It's one of the wonders of the world. That said, this is one excursion where a good level of fitness is mandatory. The climb to the top is steady in incline; there are many steps and the path well trodden. If you have average fitness you should have no worries about making it to the Abbey at the top and enjoy the splendid views.

Mont-St-Michel from the mainland

The Excursion

It will take up to three hours of driving each way to get to the island from **Le Havre**. Beginning with a drive across the amazing **Pont de Normandie** (at the time of building in 1995 this was the longest cable-stayed bridge in the world), it's a pleasant journey through the French countryside. A stop for lunch before crossing over the causeway (soon to be a bridge) to the island will give you some good photographic opportunities. Upon arrival on the island you will begin a steady walk upwards – and upwards and upwards - following the same route as pilgrims who have traversed these paths and steps since the 12th century. You'll pass many souvenir shops as well as an eatery that boasts that the omelet was invented there.

The **Abbey** is built on three levels and gives splendid views from any of these. Under the direction of a guide you can visit the church, the cloisters, and the refectory where entertaining of the nobility occurred. There are vaulted rooms, staircases and the largest fireplaces you'll ever see. It's all a bit of a maze; so go armed with a map as it is very easy to get lost. Depending on the tides surrounding the island your photographs can be very spectacular. Wet overcast days will add a great deal of atmosphere to your visit so don't be put off by the weather. Descend carefully along the same route that you ascended, this time perhaps stopping to have a drink or purchasing another souvenir in the vicinity of **Eglise St-Pierre**. Expect to fall asleep on the coach on the way back to the ship (most of our coach passengers did). Even though there is a lot of steep climbing you'll feel really proud that you have visited this amazing national monument. It's definitely a once-in-a-lifetime special event.

My Recommendation

When you are presented with an opportunity to visit such a wondrous place, and you are fit enough to walk to the top, you should not say no. On the day I did this excursion there were also day trips into Paris on offer. Of course, if you haven't seen Paris then even a few hours there is seriously tempting. You must see and enjoy Paris before you die, but don't underestimate the amazing Mont-St-Michel.

Cloisters of the Abbey

LISBON, Portugal

To appreciate Lisbon you need to spend time in both the old city as well as take a trip to the nearby countryside. In the city you should walk and ride the old tourist trams, and on any excursion to the country make sure it includes **Sintra**.

Tourist trams in Lisbon

The Excursion

The one I did took some seven hours and it showed me a diverse range of Portuguese history both ancient and modern, and a range of their customs. We began by visiting the **Belem Tower** from which Portuguese explorers departed to find and exploit new worlds. Nearby is the **Monument to the Discoveries** that celebrates the 500th anniversary of the death of Prince Henry the Navigator. Look behind you and you will see **Pont 25 de Abril,** a suspension bridge built in 1966. It has great similarities to the Golden Gate Bridge in San Francisco.

After a brief visit to the 16th century **Jeronimos Monastery**, we follow the coast road to the seaside holiday resort of Cascais. This stretch of the coast is the vacation centre for the Portuguese - with heavy traffic, beach houses, hotels, large villas, swimmers, dog walkers and hordes of tourists enjoying the sunshine. A stop in **Cascais** for refreshments is delightful as the homes are up-market, historic and their gardens well established. You will see lovely examples of ceramic tiling everywhere you look including on the public buildings - and a fine view of the harbor. Beyond Cascais the coastline has been left relatively rugged and wild. Your tour turns inland and through the low hills to **Cabo da Roca**. Here you will join a throng of tourists for a short walk to the very western end of Europe. Beyond the horizon is America. This is the only place I've been to where the tourist coaches are so numerous that full-time parking officers are employed to keep the coaches moving at a frantic arrival and departure pace. You won't have long here so don't delay in getting to the viewing area and the lighthouse.

After this it's a leisurely drive higher up into the hills to **Sintra** where, after a brief introduction, you will be given shopping time. Sintra is a delightful hill town famed for its unusual and rather large chimneys. You'll also be able to purchase lovely porcelain at much better prices than is generally offered in Lisbon and of genuine artistic quality rather than the ubiquitous tourist knock-off copies found in many of the city's tourist shops. Our tour then provided a communal meal at a family-run hotel just out of Sintra. The variety of local foods included cheese, breads, a pork and beans-type of casserole, a lemon scented rice dish called *Arroz doce* and of course, a selection of local wines. We arrived back at the ship late in to the evening having had a wonderfully diverse day of food, places and history.

To walk in the old city of Lisbon take the ship shuttle coach which will invariably drop you at **Praca da Figueira**. Here you can firstly take a tourist tram that will meander for an hour or so through the most narrow, interesting and totally absorbing hilly areas of the old city. If you have a video camera, this unique travel method will give your audiences back home a wonderful sense of being there. After your return to the square, simply amble through the monumental triumphal arch of the **Praco do Comercio** to begin your shopping in the **Rua Augusta** and the **Baixa**.

My Recommendation
Lisbon is a delightful city though its sightseeing highlights are a little spread out. You can have the best of both worlds if your cruise itinerary allows it.

That is, a well-organized and interesting excursion that includes the city, the seaside and hilltop areas. And then you can do your own thing easily, safely and with enormous enjoyment by strolling the old city centre. You should try the local wines and foods, and purchase something that is ceramic. You'll long admire it when you get it home and you'll be reminded of a wonderful city and a few hours of memorable touring.

The lovely hilltop town of Sintra

MESSINA (Taormina), Sicily, Italy

Sicily should be on everyone's bucket list of places to visit. You rarely hear a word spoken against the island and almost without fail you'll be told how special is the tourist resort of **Taormina**. The town is small, with an amazing location and in all ways, just a sheer delight to amble around. It has inspired countless writers and artists including Goethe, Richard Wagner, John Steinbeck and Woody Allen. This is where D.H. Lawrence wrote his infamous *Lady Chatterley's Lover*.

Teatro Antico Di Taormina (Greek Theatre)

The Excursion

My cruise ship berthed at **Messina**, so the excursion
to **Taormina** was a only a 45-minute coach ride
through the Sicilian countryside and coastline - with
of course, **Mt Etna** rising to dominate the landscape.
When we exited the coach we entered the town via a
descent in a huge elevator – a feeling very much of
going to a different world. As the doors opened we
saw through the ancient archway the lovely cobbled
main street. In the early morning sunshine the walls
glowed with warm ochre hues, while the local
inhabitants chatted with one another and made
preparations for the tourist visitors. A special moment
I remember is observing the local priest in deep but
humorous conversation with one of his flock, an
elderly lady. It reminded me of how important faith
and religion are in this part of the world. (At the
entrance to the port of Messina there is a wonderful
golden statue of **Madonnina del Porto** that
welcomes and says farewell to seafarers – another
reminder of the strength of faith and spirit).

After walking past the **Palazzo Corvaia** and viewing
the fountain in the **Piazza Duomo** (1635), and
passing the wonderful shops filled with liquers, cakes,
icecreams, pottery and ceramics we reached the
Greek Theatre, the **Teatro Antico Di Taormina**. Its
stunning location overlooks the beach far below and
there is **Mt Etna** in the background. In the days after
our visit Liza Minnelli was performing there, so I can
only imagine how wonderful a summer evening
listening to music or a play would be at that location.
After some shopping time the coach returns to the

ship without taking you anywhere else. We didn't get down to beach level and that was a pity, as that would have added greatly to our knowledge and appreciation of the area.

My Recommendation

Taormina will very likely, cast a spell over you. It's small and intimate compared with many other towns that cruise ships visit and this is part of its special charm. If you can combine a visit here with additional aspects of Sicily then do so. You may be very surprised at how charmed you will be with not only this town but with the whole island and its rich culture and history.

A quiet side street in Taormina

NAPLES (Pompeii and/or Isle of Capri), Italy

Excursions from a cruise ship berthed in Naples generally means time in Naples city, a visit to the ruins of **Pompeii** or a trip by ferry or hydrofoil out to the **Isle of Capri.**

Port of Naples

The Excursion

On my first visit to **Naples** I chose **Pompeii**, as a visit here is to step back in time. The ruins are so varied, so intact and so interesting that by the end of your visit, you should have a wonderful sense of what ancient Roman life was really like. But three warnings:

(1) As part of this visit you'll probably spend some 45 minutes at a cameo (or some similar)

factory, a considerable amount of time that would be better spent at the ruins.

(2) Don't expect to see all of the ruins. Today will be a good serving of them, but there is more to see than what is offered in the generally tightly explored area that the tour guides show you. (You will probably miss the remains of the House of the Gladiators (much of which collapsed in 2010) and the amphitheatre, as they are away from the general guided area).

(3) During the summer season the ruins are one of the most visited sites on earth. So expect it to be busy with coach loads of other tourists. In winter the site can be almost deserted.

If you are adventurous and take a local train to see Pompeii under your own initiative, then you will see more than on a guided tour. And don't forget to wear good sturdy walking shoes – the rough streets are very uneven and contain countless rocks and cobblestone type areas. That said, once you get past the gross commercialism at the entrance, the ruins quickly work their ancient spell on you. You are transported back in time. As you walk into the remains of a villa or a marketplace shop or the brothel you'll wish that the walls could tell you the countless stories of the lives that were lived within them. You'll see wonderful decoration in the **House of the Vettii,** the frescoes in the communal bathhouse and the lavish lifestyle lived in the **House of the Faun**. All the time on the site you will be guided, so don't expect any free time except for a few minutes at the souvenir stalls before boarding the coach for the return to the ship. If you do this as a morning excursion you may have time to visit the **Museo Archeologico Nazionale** in Naples in the afternoon. This museum contains a huge number of artifacts that were removed from Pompeii during the excavations.

On my second visit to Naples I chose the **Isle of Capri**. I had to forego my booking as I was ill that day, but my fellow cruisers who did go had the most wonderful excursion, beginning with a 45-minute hydrofoil journey to the famed (by Noel Coward) and picturesque, **Piccolo Marina**. Then by mini-bus for a 10-minute ride up the hill to the village of **Capri**. (The alternative is to wait for the funicular but the wait is often interminable as the island is always extremely popular with day visitors). The delightful town of Capri commands views of the harbor and of Naples in the distance. From there it's a walk along narrow walkways to the other side of the island to view the sparkling waters and the host of magnificent boats at anchor there.

After lunch it's back into the mini-bus (very cramped for anyone with long legs) for the hair-raising ride to the higher town of **Anacapri.** The road is very narrow and clings to the side of the mountain. Not easy for anyone with a fear of heights. Anacapri is a delight and there is shopping time here as an alternative to taking a flying fox ride to the very top of the rock. The mini-bus ride back down to the hydrofoil can be accompanied by rollicking loud Neapolitan music perhaps as my source described it "to distract us from the thoughts of careering out into the beautiful abyss of the island scenery".

My Recommendation

Walking within Naples city is interesting, but be very aware of the pickpockets and the possibility of some personal danger. If you choose Pompeii, then you are going to one of the world's greatest archeological sites. You won't see everything but you'll be fascinated by everything you do see. It's a very special excursion. If you choose Capri on a sunny day you'll be in a very crowded location. Spectacular it certainly is, but be prepared that the journey on the island might be a little more thrilling and gravity defying than you might be used to. Some full day tours will combine both Pompeii and the Isle of Capri, but that is a big day of being on the move so I suggest that you choose one or the other.

Exploring Pompeii

SALERNO (Amalfi), Italy

By far the best way to visit the fabulous **Amalfi Coast** is to arrive from the sea. In this way you are looking upwards at the amazing populated cliffs wondering how builders were able to construct so many houses and villas on what seems impossible terrain. You also see the roadway that straddles the cliffs and you should know from the excursion brochure that if you travel by road, particularly in summer, then you are very likely to be caught in an immense traffic jam going nowhere. The town also has small alleyways and lots of steps, so be sure that you are fit enough to undertake such steps and stairs. **Amalfi** is a UNESCO World Heritage Site. Pack a hat, towel, bathing suit, sunscreen and if you are prone, seasickness tablets or motion-sickness arm bands.

Amalfi Coast

The Excursion

My excursion began directly from the ship berthed at **Salerno** (not a frequently visited port by cruise ships). Our cruiser took some 40-minutes to travel along the coast to the town of **Amalfi.** Spectacular views of the coastline were intermingled with the passing sea traffic of fishing boats, yachts and luxury cruising vessels. We were headed for Amalfi, the largest town on this coast, but **Sorrento** and **Positano** would have been equally enjoyable towns to visit. At Amalfi you can visit the **Cathedral of St Andrew** (57 steps to get to the entrance) and it is said to contain some of the Apostles' remains. Browse the alleyways looking for limoncello, the speciality liqueur drink of the area, shop in the piazza, sit beside the **Fontana del Popolo**, visit the **Paper Museum** and the **Arsenal of the Maritime Republic**, walk to the beach, have a swim, have lunch. And take lots of photos.

My Recommendation

Do visit by sea. It takes all the stress out of arriving and departure, and gives you splendid views that land-based transport can't give you. It's a small town so you will have time to be indulgent with food, drink and relaxation. It's not so much of a town to see things as a town that will give you a taste of the good life. Relax and unwind before the next busy day of your vacation or recover from yesterday's hectic schedule. Either way you will benefit from today's relaxed pace.

ST PETERSBURG, Russia

When you first sail in to the port you'll wonder what lies beyond the communist-built apartment blocks and the isolated location of the port facilities. Believe me you are in for a treat. Most of the cruise lines have a blanket visa arrangement for their passengers to go ashore as part of the organized ship excursions so this means that at all times you will be captive to the tour leader on your excursion. They are responsible for your care and to return you to the ship. They take this responsibility very seriously and you therefore won't have any free time to go shopping or exploring on your own. It's a leave-the-ship, stay-as-a-group, return-to-the-ship coach tour. You need to have your own visa organized many months in advance if you want to see anything in St Petersburg on your own. Having said that, you will feel very safe even if you don't speak a word of Russian and you will see magnificent and grand buildings that will stay in your memory long after you return home.

Peterhof

The Excursion(s)

This city offers many outstanding and magnificent attractions. Most cruise lines stay for 36 hours so make this a visit to remember. In other cities a half-day tour is often all you need, but here you need to be on the go the entire time you are berthed. Prepare yourself that it *will* be exhausting, but oh, so very worth it. If it's your first visit to this city this is *not* the time to stay on the ship.

When visiting many of the sites you will be required to pay a photography fee to your guide – for *each* site. It varies, but around $US5 for still photos and up to $US15 for video would be usual, and this must be paid in American cash – no credit cards – and no change given. You get a colored sticker placed on the front of your camera, and believe me you will be confronted by a very dour Russian female guard if you even attempt to take a photo without having a sticker in place. They are serious about this so don't think that you will get away without paying.

The Hermitage Museum - arguably this is one of the biggest and best art museums in the world. Even if you have only a passing interest in art this is a treasure not to be ignored. Its 353 rooms house works from **Michelangelo, Leonardo da Vinci, Titian, Raphael, the French Impressionists,** as well as glassware, jewellery, statues, etc, etc. Over three million items all told, so expect to be taken on a guided tour that will only show you the crème-de-la-crème of the exhibits. In summer it will be crowded, hard to see the works without hordes of others getting in the way, and with very little time to linger to deeply appreciate the works. And all of this is within spectacular staircases, grand vistas of room after room, amazing floor and ceiling decorations and incredible chandeliers. The Czars who originally lived there knew a thing or two about magnificence to impress. Photographers, keep a watchful eye for splendid panoramic views from the upper windows, as these views will not be pointed out to you. Sometimes these can surpass the art on display in that area.

One warning: pickpockets! Take very little of value with you on this excursion, hold on to everything and be conscious of your possessions – all of the time. Passports and wallets get stolen on a daily basis so make no mistake, be serious about guarding your passport and keep an alert eye out for the safety of your fellow travelers in the group.

Peterhof - this is **Peter the Great's Summer Palace** - a grand palace approximately an hour's drive from the ship. You pass through the suburbs before arriving at the palace. Tours of the interior take approximately an hour and there are no cameras allowed inside the palace itself. (These, along with handbags and backpacks have to be lodged at the free cloakroom facility before the tour commences). Outside at 11am the ornamental fountains are turned on to the sound of a grand musical fanfare. To see the sparkling waters and the gold covered statues is a stunning combination of opulence and beauty. Everyone crowds in to this area at this time, so again, hold on to your valuables as we were warned that pickpockets do frequent the crowds who are all distracted taking photographs. Your guide will then walk you through some of the magnificent gardens and other fountains before walking you towards the sea. Many tours include a fast 30-minute hydrofoil journey back to St Petersburg. If yours does, take it, as the arrival into St Petersburg by water is memorable. The buildings and the movement and diversity of the water traffic combine to give a glimpse into the soul of what has made St Petersburg a centre of art and commerce.

Church of the Spilled Blood - if you want photos of a quintessential iconic Russian church, then this is not to be missed. The entire church, both inside and out - that's some 23,000 square feet - is covered in small mosaic tiles. The result is nothing short of breathtaking. From the outside you'll see the richly decorated onion domes and on the inside you will stand and wonder at the ability and dedication of artisans to undertake such a monumental task. You'll need to pay for taking photographs, and again, the pickpockets are in attendance, so be careful of all your valuables whilst you are diverted looking at the walls.

A Ballet Performance at the Mariinsky Theater and **A Folkloric Spectacular** are also offered as excursions, as is the magnificent **Catherine's Palace**. The advice we were given from other passengers is that the ballet and the folk dancing were very entertaining, very Russian but coming after the long day of touring some found it hard to stay awake. And then there was the inevitable early start for the next tour the next morning. Through lack of time I opted for not seeing Catherine's Palace as I'd already seen the Schonbrunn Palace in Vienna, and was advised that they were very similar.

My Recommendation

Be prepared for a wonderfully rich, spectacular, diverse and exhausting day and a half cultural experience that will inevitably enrich your life for years to come. Of all the ports you can visit, this is definitely not one where you should stay on the ship. Be brave, appreciate there will be crowds and constant organization, but above all embrace grandeur, a long past opulent but violent era the remains of which we can only marvel at - and appreciate that through the joys of travel, that we can come in peace to understand an alternative culture to that of our own.

Detail on the Church of the Spilled Blood

STOCKHOLM, Sweden

I spent many happy days here following a Baltic cruise. As the ship berthed at an early hour I took an orientation excursion that filled the morning and got us to our hotel by early afternoon. You realize that even though the city is on 14 islands, everything is connected by bridges and within easy walking distances. Do an organized city-explorer excursion and then go explore on foot yourself. If it's summer it's still light until nearly 11pm and that gives you a lot more exploring time.

Bicycles and boats in Stockholm

The Excursion

From the cruise ship we drove through the leafy **Djurgarden** park area, past the various consulates and to the amazing **Vasa Museum.** This purpose-built museum houses a massive warship that sank in the harbor on its maiden voyage in 1628. After centuries encased in mud, it has been restored and is on display. You can see into it (but not go on it) from

six different levels. It is nothing short of amazing.
The area is very dark, so photography can be difficult.
We then traveled around the city stopping at various
viewing areas before being left at a central hotel from
which we hailed a cab to our own accommodation.

Other places of interest in this stylish, safe and very
clean city include:

Skansen – this area, just up the street from the Vasa
Museum, contains 150 original old buildings
collected from all over Sweden. It's a huge open-air
museum that gives a very interesting look into the
Swedish heritage. Artisans dressed in traditional
costume demonstrate their skills, there's a wonderful
children's zoo along with plenty of areas for picnics
or places to purchase food. Some good views of
Stockholm can be had from the higher reaches. Go
there by traditional tram – it's great fun.

The Royal Palace – fascinating to look through, but
most tourists are there for the changing of the guard at
noon. In summer this is a very crowded courtyard but
there are enough soldiers, bandsmen and horses to
make the event a colorful and enjoyable photographic
opportunity. Be there at least 30 minutes beforehand
to stake a good viewing position. Afterwards wander
the narrow back streets and enjoy a meal or browse
the many handicraft shops.

Cruise – there are all manner of water vessels plying
the waters around the islands. Any one of them will
give you a great perspective of the city and its

uniqueness. Keep an eye out for the island where the pop group Abba produced much of their music.

My Recommendation

My impression of the city before my visit was that it looked from the maps, to be very spread out, and difficult to get from one place to another. In fact, everything is quite compact, interconnected and with a combination of trams and walking you can see all the main attractions without difficulty. The hop-on, hop-off bus is ideal if you want to go exploring by yourself, though you'll soon realize that all the main attractions are in fact, very close to one another and a bus is possibly not all that necessary. Remember that sturdy shoes are required to counteract the many cobblestones.

Hot air balloons drift on a Stockholm summer evening

TALLINN, Estonia

This medieval old town is one of the finest in Europe – and the good news is that it is still relatively undiscovered by the hordes of tourists found elsewhere in Western Europe. Every Baltic cruise ship stops here for a day so there can be a couple of ships in port on any one day but it is not crowded. Its claim to fame to the outside world is that the Internet telephone service Skype had a lot of its development realized here.

The Old Town, Tallinn

The Excursion

After a leisurely drive through the modern city to the base of the ancient wall that protected the city, you walk along the winding cobblestone streets to the **Palace Square** and then onto **Town Hall Square.** Here you will have time to do some souvenir shopping, before another walk down the hill to where your coach will be waiting. The shops are filled with wonderful handicrafts and babushka (or nesting) dolls of every possible color and creation. This is a good city in which to purchase these items both for quality and price.

Then it's on the coach for a short journey to the city outskirts to visit the **Rocca al Mare Open-Air Museum**. After all the other cities you might have seen on your vacation, this museum is a breath of calmness and sanity. Set in glorious woodland, original houses, barns, windmills etc have all been relocated from various parts of Estonia and rebuilt here. There is a lot of space between each of the buildings so walking in the peaceful surroundings of the forest is a sheer delight. There are also demonstrations of dancing (held outside in the open air) and intricate embroidery. Also horse and cart rides and you will probably get the opportunity to try their traditional cake with your tea or coffee. The souvenir shop offers excellent hand-made items.

My Recommendation
This is a walking tour that is filled with interest and not at any fast pace. Both aspects of the excursion offer a jaded vacationer a breath of fresh air and an upliftment for the soul. It's enriching and restorative to have a feeling that you are discovering something wonderful that the rest of the world hasn't yet caught up with. Tallinn is now one of my very favorite cities.

VALETTA, Malta

Your day will most likely begin with your arrival into one of the most spectacular harbors in the world. This arrival is well worth getting up early for. You pass the occasional small fishing boat, the sun begins to rise above the horizon and there in front of you is the fort-like grandeur of **Valetta**, its sandstone walls glowing golden in the morning light. Today will be a step back into history to the world of knights, conquerors, palaces and cathedrals.

Arriving in Valetta

The Excursion

The excursion takes place in two parts – it begins with a short coach ride into the city of **Valetta** where you disembark for a walking tour. On the way to **St. John's Co-Cathedral** you will pass the outside of the **Grand Master's Palace** (which is now the

Parliament) and visit the **Barracca Gardens**. From this high point you will be able to take spectacular photos of your ship, the **Three Cities** and **Fort Ricasoli.** Walking through the narrow sun-drenched streets you'll feel a million miles away from your everyday life at home. These streets feel ancient, and the life lived behind the walls hints at historical intrigue and mystery. At the stunning Cathedral built by the famed Knights Of Malta in 1572 don't miss seeing the huge painting *The Beheading of Saint John The Baptist* painted by Caravaggio in 1608 (no photos allowed). After a short shopping stop in the area of the Cathedral it's onto the coach and into the dry, almost treeless countryside to the old capital, **Mdina**.

Mdina I found was a stunning example of a medieval walled city that is still in active use today (some 300 people currently live there). It's a walking city where you will again be transported back to another time. After entering through the very imposing **Mdina Gate** and beyond the walls, you'll find fascinating shops, squares, various palazzos and monasteries and with the impressive **St Paul's Cathedral** at the heart. I enjoyed photographing the very many impressive doors along our walking route, the decorative items on the various buildings and capturing the golden colors of the sunlit narrow medieval streets. And I wanted to stay much longer than the tour allowed. So my advice to photographers is to photograph as much as you can as the tour progresses and not leave it until your short period of shopping time. This is a walled city that is beautifully preserved, with a fascinating history and a living presence rarely found elsewhere.

My Recommendation

Mdina has become one of my most treasured excursion memories. The glowing sun-drenched images of my photographs speak to me of a history that is almost tangible, still living and impressive - of a people who have done it hard in life, who have lived a history against all the harsh physical elements and numerous invaders - of a city far removed from my own suburban existence. Take a tour of these two cities and you will experience history like few other places can match.

Glorious building in Mdina

VENICE, Italy

Your day here should live in your vacation memory as one of those very special times that quite simply can't be replicated anywhere else on earth. Venice is unique and an absolute 'must' to visit. The ship will berth on the edge of the city. This means that you will need to be transported by small cruiser to **St Mark's Square** to begin your main walking explorations (approximately a 20-minute water journey).

A quiet Venetian canal

The Excursion

You will arrive and/or depart Venice by sea and therefore enjoy one of the great views of this earth – Venice across its rooftops. Nowhere in the city can come close to giving non-cruising visitors this stunning view. It's a remarkable perspective on this ancient city. Before you passes all the hustle and bustle of the city, the myriad water traffic, the **Doge's Palace** and **St Mark's Square**. It's a view to never tire of, so make sure you're in position to take some of the best photographs of your entire vacation.

Venice is a city that you need to partially explore on your own and partially be escorted through. I was keen to see the islands nearby so from the ship our cruiser took us down the fascinating **Canale di San Marco** and past **St Mark's Square.** If you missed photographing the southern side of the canal on the sail in, then this is a great opportunity to take photos, especially if you have a telephoto lens. Then it's out into the peaceful **Lagoon** for a 30-minute boat ride to the islands of **Murano** (where you will see glass-blowing and amazing glass products available for sale) then on to **Burano,** a tranquil fishing and lace-making village. Keep that camera handy as the houses here are all multi-colored and they make memorable photographic subjects. These islands make a wonderful contrast to the hustle of the main city area and are a good place to make purchases of better quality and value than can easily be found in the city.

We return then to **St Mark's Square** and it's wise to have your guide introduce you to some of the sights.

Make sure that you don't leave the tour leader without having a map of the city in your hand. If you go exploring yourself you are sure to lose your way at some time or other – it's incredibly easy but good fun to do. It's an easy walk to the **Bridge of Sighs, the Doge's Palace, the Grand Canal, St Mark's Basilica, the Rialto Bridge, the Peggy Guggenheim Museum** and to the back corner of St Mark's Square where you can catch a **gondola** for that quintessential Venetian experience. To be drifting on a gondola down the narrow canals whilst someone is singing is one of life's tingle-in-the-spine moments. Treat yourself to this and it will be a lifetime memory. If you'd like an alcoholic drink it's a short walk to the original **Harry's Bar** where you can rub shoulders with the ghosts of the world's most famous artists and writers. If you prefer a coffee in St Mark's Square be aware that prices can blow a big hole in your vacation budget. It's one of the world's most expensive places to sit and sip.

As you will be given, time to do your own thing, be very sure of where and at what time to meet your excursion boat to take you back to the ship. Miss this and it will be expensive and difficult to get back to the cruise ship. Also don't underestimate how easy it is to be so absorbed in the back canals of the city so that when it's time to return you have no idea how to get back to the meeting point. Keep that map firmly in your hand. Also remember that there are numerous Feast days celebrated in this part of Italy and perhaps like me on my second day there, you'll find central Venice closed for business. On the bright side of that there are still many souvenir shops open – and there's less crowding whilst walking.

My Recommendation

Discovering Venice on foot and by waterway is to see a fantastic world where every photo you've ever seen of the city comes magically to life. It's one city that is every bit as dramatic, colorful, curious and enriching as you have always imagined. The sights and discoveries that you see through your own eyes will become special to you and will be long remembered. Venice is a once in a lifetime experience that lives up to every piece of hype you've ever heard or seen about it. Have a fantastic day there.

A gondola is awaiting your pleasure

VILLEFRANCHE (Monaco/Nice), France

You can do a very pleasant half-day tour to either Monaco or Nice, or see both over the course of a day. Most likely you will anchor off **Villefranche** and come in to shore by tender. This places you approximately half-way between the two areas. If you want to see the inside of the **Casino** at **Monte Carlo** then you need to do an afternoon excursion, as the Casino does not open until 2pm Monday to Friday, and noon on Saturdays and Sundays.

Harbor at Monaco

The Excursion

I opted for the **Monte Carlo** and **Monaco** experience, Monte Carlo being one of the four Quarters on the Monaco principality. Your journey there will as likely as not, be bathed in sunshine, with wonderful sea views in between extraordinary villas and lush flowering vegetation. This is the spotlessly clean world of millionaires and billionaires, where money and style speak volumes and where at times it will feel like an offshoot of a fantasy theme park. All coach visits are tightly controlled and coaches must park in a huge undercover parking area where you will disembark and take an elevator to a higher level at the top of **the Rock**.

From this area it's a short walk to the **Prince's Palace of Monaco** - past the **Oceonographic Museum**, a few minutes stop at the **Cathedral** to pay your respects at the tomb of Princess Grace (the actress Grace Kelly) and then a short stroll through the delightful area of the old town. There are splendid photos of the opulence of Monaco to be taken from both sides of the Palace forecourt. You may also see the changing of the guard (a three-person event, so don't be expecting a spectacle). After this shopping and photographic time, it's back down the hill to the coach for a short drive to another parking area within a short walk of the Casino. On this drive you'll see part of the course used for the Formula One Grand Prix car racing circuit.

Outside the Casino (the **Place du Casino**) are immaculate gardens and high-end shops, the grand **Hotel de Paris** and what I regard as a stunning piece of Belle Epoque architecture, **Brasserie Le Café de Paris**. This is an area where you will feel that you have been transported to a magical enchanted fantasy world. Be prepared for high prices for anything you eat or drink, but if you would like a taste of total luxury this is the ideal place to indulge. It would certainly remain as a highlight of any vacation. If you wish to try your luck at the Casino remember that a dress code applies (smart casual through to glamour) and there is a 10 Euro admission. After time here, it's a return coach ride along a different roadway (**Corniche**) to the ship terminal, again passing magnificent views and stunning homes. Today has been class all the way.

Everywhere on the **Cote d'Azur** there are interesting things to see and a lot of visual interest getting there and back. You could enjoy visits to:

Nice – walk the **Promenade des Anglais** with its fine and elegant hotels (especially the **Hotel Negresco**), shops and eating places. Pick up a bargain at the **Outdoor Market**, explore the **Old City** area with its wonderful shopping within the winding narrow streets or for a museum there's the **Musee Matisse, Musee Chagall** and the **Musee d'Art Contemporain** (for Pop Art). To view works by the French Impressionists then visit either the **Musee des Beaux Arts** and/or the **Palais Massena**.

Cannes – home of the famed film festival. Interesting beach, lovely old hotels and places to eat, stylish French Riviera location.

Grasse – this is where the French perfume industry began and a visit to the perfume factory is an extraordinary opportunity to test and understand the process. Your credit card could get scorched here. Many tours also call in to **Eze** where there is a splendid view of the whole coastline.

St. Paul de Vence – a 16th century walled village with lovely views, narrow streets filled with art and souvenir shops and a copy of Rodin's famous sculpture *The Thinker*.

My Recommendation

Any excursion along the Cote d'Azur will be interesting as there are so many places that we hear about in the news and where celebrities like to vacation. Personally, Monaco is a standout highlight with Nice a close second. Try to take a tour that will give you time to peruse the shops even if you aren't buying, time for a relaxed meal whilst you watch the amazing lifestyle pass your table and try not to fit too much in to one day – it is a relaxed vacation after all. Be aware that in the height of the summer tourist season the roads can be very slow – another good reason not to do too much distance in one day.

Port of Villefranche

Do-It-Yourself Cities

There are some cities of Europe that lend themselves to being explored on foot without the need for a tour guide. They are compact enough to be easily explored in less than a day or even within a morning or an afternoon. Here are three of them that are additional to earlier notes on other specific cities where you perhaps need to have an organized excursion and then do your own thing.

They are all old towns where every corner yields another fascinating photograph, every doorway is a portal to an historic past and every cobblestone has had a million feet pass over its surface. You will lose your sense of direction, you'll be fascinated by the variety of shops, you'll see everyday life going on about you and you'll sense a history that has been silently written into every building.

With a good map in hand, maybe a GPS device or an electronic tablet where you have previously downloaded maps and information, set out with your traveling companion and enjoy your day. It will be the unexpected that will delight you and give you memories to cherish.

Know how you will get back to the ship and allow additional time to do so. Remember you are on your own and not part of an organized ship tour - and the ship will leave without you if you are late.

Have a wonderful and memorable day as you explore....

AJACCIO, Corsica, France

Typical street scene in Ajaccio

Be prepared to fall in love with this small city. It's not yet been overrun by the tourist hordes and is therefore a delight to amble around even in the height of summer. The ship will dock within easy strolling distance of the main shops and beachfront. It's a wonderful mixture of French, Italian and North African architecture, streets lined with palm trees, the sounds of the French language being spoken, beaches and historic buildings. Things to see include the **Musee Fesch** with its impressive collection of Italian paintings, **Place de Gaulle** with a huge statue of Napoleon, **Cours Napoleon** with its many clothing boutiques and eateries, **Place Foch** (including another statue of Napoleon), the **Rue Bonaparte** which gives access to the old town, and of course, the birthplace of Napoleon, **Maison Bonaparte**. Nearby are the **Cathedral** and the **St Erasmus Jesuit Church.** You'll have the most pleasant, safe and delightful day just walking, soaking up the atmosphere and watching the world pass by whilst enjoying coffee and those magnificent French pastries. Bon appetite!

This is a day on your vacation to let the soul be rested and revived and to let your head be relieved of taking in ever more facts and historical dates.

A cruise ship view of the waterfront at Ajaccio

AMSTERDAM, The Netherlands

Amsterdam canal

Any ship-offered excursion to old Amsterdam will include two things – glass-blowing and a canal cruise. My advice is to get yourself into the old city with a good map in hand, wear sturdy walking shoes as there are a lot of cobblestones, and you will easily see everything you want to see. You don't even have to be adventurous to do this here.

Firstly take an hour-long **canal cruise**. This will show you many of the sights and offer lots of wonderful photographic opportunities. Unfortunately in no way will it help you get your bearings. Expect to get lost in the old city. It's part of the day and you seriously can't go very wrong before you'll locate on the map where you are. Use the tramline to assist you in locating the sights.

After the canal cruise there is a lot of choices of things to see - **Anne Frank's House, Rembrandt's House, the Red Light District,** the high bell tower of the **Westerkerk, the Rijks Museum** with many paintings from the Dutch Masters and just a little further along the street the wonderful **Van Gogh Museum** (always extremely busy but a joy to visit). Visit the **Flower Market,** amble the canals and take more wonderful photographs. And for a unique Amsterdam photo look to the left-hand side of the **Central Railway Station** and see the huge bike racks holding thousands of the ubiquitous black cycles. If you're in Amsterdam overnight then check out the classical music being played at the famous **Concertgebouw** concert hall. Hearing anything played live there is a musical treat.

Above all, old Amsterdam is a walking city and whatever the season, it has a rich character and texture. And don't be alarmed that you can see right into people's homes any time of the day and observe them living their life. It's very accepted locally though possibly not what you are used to back home. Have a joyous and fascinating day discovering everything for yourself.

DUBROVNIK, Croatia

View from the top of the city walls

Take the ship's shuttle coach in to the old walled city and enjoy a few hours wandering the shops and along the top of the **city walls**. The city is a UNESCO World Heritage site and is very easy to explore. Be warned though that in summer the heat can be very intense through to unbearable – and that can also be said of the tourist crowds. Keep hydrated and wear a wide brimmed hat. Also be aware that walking the wall can be extremely hot and tiresome and there are few places to exit. Other times of the year the weather is much more pleasant.

The views of the ocean, **St John's Fort** and the red roofs of the city make the effort very worthwhile. At ground level look for the **Rector's Palace, Minceta**

Tower, Onofrio's Fountain, Stradun (the main thoroughfare), **Sponza Palace, Orlando's Column, Luza** and the **City-Bell Tower, Major Council Palace** and the **City Guard Building**. There are shops and cafes galore, market stalls and a lot of evidence in the walls that this is a city with a recent turbulent past. You might also consider a cable car ride that will give you stunning panoramic views of the walled city.

Food market held within the city walls

An inexpensive and natural method of reducing the effects of nausea from sea or motion sickness

This is the true story of how my use of acupressure wrist-bands for traveling has opened up the world to me - and I'd like to share it with you in the hope that it may also be useful to you or your loved ones. They can be purchased on all cruise ships or in advance at local pharmacies and drugstores.

I have been one of the world's worst sailors! I've been ill on 50,000 tons of cruise ship before it even left the harbor (Sydney Harbor). But nowadays I cruise the world. I love being pampered. I love the continuous eating and entertainment cruise ships provide. I love seeing new ports of call. And all this is now possible for me because of those two little acupressure buttons on my wrist-band. Wearing them is such a small price to pay for nausea-free travel. And the confidence they give me to go anywhere and do anything around water is quite simply, fantastic.

Decades after that ill-fated cruise I discovered acupressure wrist-bands, and suddenly the wonderful world of water travel opened up to me. Cruising the high seas, yachting, small fishing boats, river cruising, it was now all possible – without debilitating nausea and that horrible, horrible, horrible "wish I was dead" feeling.

But it didn't stop there. On my various coach trips when I had to sit at the rear of the bus or over a wheel, and especially on winding mountain roads, I used the bands. No motion sickness – just the pleasure of the journey and seeing exciting new places.

I also like to sit at the rear of large planes, and that can sometimes mean a little more turbulence. So I put on the wrist-bands, have a great flight and then remove them as soon as I have landed.

Similarly, if I'm a backseat passenger in a car, slipping on the wrist-bands assures me of a pleasant journey.

As I love the freedom to travel – and more importantly, to enjoy that travel, I always carry additional sets of wrist bands with me as you can be a wonderful savior to your fellow travelers by offering a set to those who are beginning to feel nauseous. Of course, they work best if used from before the journey begins, but even after early symptoms occur it's often not too late to stabilize the condition. You can be sure that the next time they travel they will use the wrist-bands from *before* the journey begins to be sure of having a nausea-free journey. Your act of kindness of giving them wrist-bands and teaching them the ease of using them won't quickly be forgotten. I have several friends and travel companions who continually thank me for 'saving' their vacation by having introduced them to acupressure wrist-bands. Wearing them yourself is also a great conversation starter as just about everyone knows of someone who could benefit from a little nausea relief whilst traveling.

Perhaps, like me, you need to have a 'trial run' with them. I was skeptical that a couple of buttons pressing on my wrist area would give me the key to embracing nausea-free cruising. My trial run was traveling by ferry across the notoriously choppy English Channel. I can't begin to describe the fantastic elation I had by half way across when I realized that I was walking the deck, watching the passing sea traffic and talking with my fellow passengers without a thought of seasickness. I pushed my belief (and new relief) even further by ordering a hamburger and eating it. I had arrived on a fantastic new level of possibility – perhaps now after 30 years of avoidance I could do that sea cruise I'd been too frightened to book.

And I did! A 10-day eastern Mediterranean cruise - and since then I've also cruised to Alaska, Hawaii, the Baltic, the Bay of Biscay and several times around the Mediterranean.

The world is my oyster. Certainly I've had my 'off color' days in very heavy seas but on no journey have I vomited. In the Mediterranean, especially in summer when the waters are calmer, sometimes I only wear the bands for the first day or so and then take them off with no ill results. I always carry them with me ready to put on 'just in case' but mostly they haven't been needed. They're also great for the shore-excursions that take place via smaller boats, barges etc. Traveling the Venetian islands by small water taxi, whale watching from a tiny boat and flying in a small seaplane in Alaska bring back memories of particularly enjoyable excursions.

Will they work for me?
I can't tell you that everyone who uses the wrist-bands will enjoy totally nausea-free travel – but it is rare that they don't assist in the alleviation of distress. Feeling as wretched as I did when traveling on water before I discovered wrist-bands I can only say that I would have tried anything rather than continue suffering that debilitating and draining nausea feeling. It's more than just hope that they will work. It's an oriental acupressure healing method that's been known for literally thousands of years. It is the same acupressure point that is used for harmonizing energy in the chest for digestion, acid regurgitation, blood flow, hiccups, belching and calming the mind. You have nothing to loose and probably everything to gain. If nausea (or the fear of nausea) is holding back your zest for living, then it's time to take action and give them a try. It's a small investment that will bring years of happy dividends.

I trust that my story may be beneficial to you and your loved ones. Happy traveling!

Peter Benn

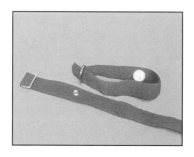

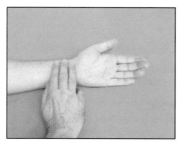

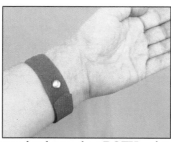

Note that bands need to be used on BOTH wrists to be effective.
Disclaimer: All advice in this publication is general in nature, and is
non-specific to individuals or groups. It should not be construed to be
medical advice. Always consult your doctor/physician before using any
form of acupressure or nausea relief device. Nausea and/or vomiting
can be a sign of a more serious medical condition and should be treated
under medical advice. If you have poor circulation, use a pacemaker or
suffer from thrombosis you should also seek medical advice before use.
If devices cause any swelling or irritation, discontinue use immediately
and seek appropriate medical advice. Wearing acupressure wrist-bands
is not a guarantee of nausea relief.

Copyright, Disclaimer and Publisher Details

Publisher Details
Published by Argosy Media
Postal: PO Box 7615, St Kilda Road, Victoria 8004 Australia
Email: videobookshelf@ozemail.com.au

ISBN: 978-1481205641

Sign near the souvenir shops at Ephesus